Bubba Heights

By

Albert John

Peebles

ALBERT JOHN PEEBLES

ALBERT JOHN PEEBLES

BUBBA HEIGHTS

^^^
^^^^^^^^^^^^^^

CAST OF CHARACTERS

1. STEVE EAGLESON
2. JAKE HANDLEY
3. OWEN AND TK BIRD
4. BOSS DARDEN
5. THE MOTORCYCLE GANG
6. PINBALL BILL
7. BECKY THORNAPPLE
8. SUSAN ROCKCREEK
9. JUDY MUDDLER
10. CITY POLICE CHIEF
11. DONNY
12. GEORGE BUCKET
13. JASON BUCKET
14. OSS BILKERS
15. SONNY

16. DOUG SLUGS
17. BUDDY MILKWEED
18. LUCY MILKWEED
19. HOSS AND BETTY WILLIAMS
20. DETECTIVE BENNY HASSLEMAN
21. JERRY FIELDS
22. GINA COLDPENNY
23. JANET
24. HENRY
25. ROSS WINDFIELD
26. HOSS
27. OTIS CRABTREE
28. FIRST AGENT
29. SECOND AGENT
30. DOUG AND JULIE

~~~~~~~~~~~~~~~~~~~~~~~~~~~~

1

BUBBA HEIGHTS

THE MOTORCYCLE GANG

On a late evening of July 15th a gang of motorcyclist from southern California is making camp in a clearing just off route one near Eureka on the coast. A group of some fifty riders are on a road trip to Seattle, Washington. The group is made up of about thirty men and twenty women. These are professional people. Mostly Lawyers and business people on a summer vacation.

After making camp and having a cook out one man says; "Hey did yo see that?" Then several small rocks suddenly came flying into the camp area. These are followed by some bigger rocks. Then a rather large rock smashes one of the motorcycles.

The group at a loss to understand all this packs up in a hurry and begins to leave as quickly as possible. Several riders have to double up because their cycles are heavily damaged. Some of the group seen what looked like giant men coming down the hill and throwing the big rocks.

Although they got out with their lives and lost a few motorcycles they pressed on as fast as possible. They made a complete police report. One of the local people told them the next morning that several colonies of the big fellows live up there in the mountains, and may have seen them as a threat.

A California cop named Steve Anderson on vacation visiting relatives in Eureka decided to have a look for himself. He drove to the area to find several destroyed motorcycles, and other things destroyed. A number of tents and equipment were left behind as well.

Steve who was born near here finds all of this very unusual, because the big creatures are not generally known to do things like this. He finds it all very strange.

Steve while having lunch talks to other local people about it, and they to find it strange; however, nothing much can be done about it. The police make a complete report, and the people who lost their bikes made insurance claims.

Still in all Steve was bothered by the whole thing, and told his dad he was going to take a leave of absence and seen what he could find out about all of this.

2

THE EARTHQUAKE

The day the event with the motorcycle gang early in the morning an earthquake shook the entire area. It was not real strong; however, it did do some damage in many places including Bubba Heights.

The radio said it was measured at 5.3 on the scale. Well from time to time quakes have rattled the northwestern part of California. A few hours later people went on with their business, and most everything got back to normal. Yet there was some cleaning up to do, and the city got right on that.

Steve was at his dad's place that night, and the house got one hell of a shaking, but there was no serious damage. In the morning he went to visit friends from school and spent the better part of that day meeting with people he knew and grew up with before leaving for the military.

People he knew introduced him to other people who lived there. He met Doug Slugs and his wife. And he was introduced to Pinball Bill and Jake, and John Crane. While visiting he also met Hoss and Betty Williams among other people.

3

THE LOST REFRIGERATOR

Every Saturday Jake goes out with Owen and TK Bird to earn a few extra bucks making deliveries or picking something up. The Saturday after Boss Bilkers started pushing up daises.

It was early and one of those mornings after a fresh rain. After they picked up this industrial refrigerator for a restaurant across town Owen made a turn faster than he should have. Then they had forgotten to tie it down.

With a loud groan it slid off the truck and sailed downhill while they slapped on the brakes. As this large appliance rolled down the street and picked up a decent speed.

Everyone was screaming and they turned the truck around and tried following it down the hill. You could hear people running and screaming.

Turns out at the bottom of the long hill were a food store and she was heading right for the front door that early morning.

Then it happened!

The refrigerator crashed into the door knocking both of them from their hinges. Then the doors went flying in different directions. With a loud crash, smoke, and debris the unit went sailing down the produce aisle with women running and screaming for their life. It destroyed the whole area.

It crashed into back of the door sailing out across the shipping dock and slowed in the back parking lot. The problem was it still had enough momentum, as the guys almost were able to get their hands on it and rolled down a grass hill. Now she was traveling at a decent speed toward the Interstate.

Suddenly brakes were screeching, and everyone was trying to get out of the way. There were four or five pile-ups. After that the big appliance groaned as it went over a retaining wall and into the ocean.

A truck skids on a hill and a big refrigerator falls out on the street taking out several cars on its way down the hill. It picks up speed takes out a police car and comes crashing into the big restaurant at the bottom.

People are running for their life as the refrigerator goes through the kitchen and out the back wall. It goes over a hill and crashed on the Interstate created a mess.

A crowd gathered to watch it float away. Soon it was gone and nobody knew where exactly. It was a bad day for a number of insurance companies, but that's why people buy insurance isn't it?

Who knows what the outcome of all of this would be?

The guys got in their truck acting like nothing had happened and went home for the day. The nightly News was asking for whoever caused this mess to turn their selves in, but all the guys did was open another beer and say, "Tomorrow is another day!"

The city police chief came out himself to make the report. He was still a bit anxious after just filing a report of the motorcycle incident. Chief Rogers has had an very interesting day.

After questioning a few people who saw the whole thing he wrote it up; however, he suspected who it was after the description given him of the truck. He had to think on this one a while, because he is friends with the family of the truck owner, and since nobody got hurt, and because there is insurance he decided to leave it alone for a while.

After all his wife Kate wouldn't want any trouble over this. Kate's sister Emily is family, and like they say, "Blood is thicker than water." Like they say; :there you have it!"

The chief drives back to his office just as the rain slows down. He walks in and says too one of the deputies; all in a day's work!

4

LIFE AT THE FACTORY

Late afternoon in the factory

Sonny get your ass over here!

What you need boss?

I need you to get your ass in gear and get that truck unloaded, replied Boss Darden.

Time is money, and Bobby Bilkers is on my butt for this stuff!

Is your brother going with us tonight?

Don't know Sonny?

He's making a late delivery. He has to drop off a refrigerator at the Lopburns over in Bubba Heights.

Well that place is up on the hill, and you know what happened the last time they made a delivery up there.

Look George I'm sure those guys know what they are doing!

Donny

Boss it's all most time to go home!

Boss Darden

So what! When did that ever mean anything around here?

Get in gear.

We don't have all day!

Just then George bucket walks over holding a mop

George

Donny we have the UFO meeting tonight! How long do you have to stay?

Donny

I'll be there. Trust me on this. I had to stop home and pick up Kathy, so I'll be a little late. Make sure you bring the photos we took out in the woods.

When they see these pictures of Bigfoot we will be stars. You know how the women love this stuff! Well we will see. Remember that gal Susan Rogers will be speaking tonight, and she actually witnessed some Bigfoot.

George

Yeah well, the UFO babes are not what you might call normal if you know what I mean, but then people say the same thing about us, so there you have it. Got to go later dude! Hey don't forget!

Donny

Forget what?

George

It's my turn to give a talk tonight!

Donny

Yeah, well all right!

LATER THAT NIGHT

THE MEETING TALKS PLACE

Becky Thornapple calls the meeting to order.

The UFO meeting is called to order in the old hotel on main Street. The place is run now buy the city who has been trying to sell it.

After the meeting is called to order and a few comments are made. The speaker calls on Susan to speak.

People are telling stories of their own experiences.

After an hour or so they take a break for coffee.

Becky

Well the meeting is good tonight. A lot of new people, and some new sightings of UFO's and Bigfoot. It's all really exciting.

The club meeting lasts for hours and Susan Roger a good looking gal, a graduate of Robert Wilfred High recites a poem she wrote about the space brothers and the environment.

SUSAN ROGERS

After a short coffee break gets up and gives her talk to the UFO group. She covers a few Bigfoot sightings and how they might be related to UFO's.

Several people give a small talk that night, and after a break they have a group discussion about the talk. Susan had seen a pair of Bigfoot creatures depart a UFO last spring and is still telling everyone about it.

Donny

He addresses the group of about thirty-five people.

I seen Bigfoot behind Tom's dinner about a month ago going through the big garbage dumpster. When he saw me he screamed and I ran for my life! I know some of you don't believe it, but if you had seen what I saw you would have ran too!

After the meeting they talked for a while about Bigfoot and other things. Next month's meeting was now on the minds of most of the people.

The club show a movie and each week someone gives a talk about UFO's, Bigfoot, or other weird things. They were planning a hike out into the mountains in early May. That is the time Bigfoot has been seen moving north in one of their annual migrations.

Around ten the meeting comes to a close and everyone leaves.

~~~~~~~~~~~~~~~~~~~~~~~~~~~~~~

5

THE NEXT DAY AT THE FACTORY

Buddy Milkweed and Jason Bucket are working loading boxes with Sunny Buckman. Boss Bilkers is standing around watching them.

Boss Bilkers

If you boys would have went to college a long time ago you might be my boss by now, but you were too lazy just like your old man.

One of the workers

Hey boss did you here what happened yesterday?

Boss Bilkers

No what?

I feel for ya all, but let's get the job done!

We don't have all day. I got a dollar waiting on a dime

here! It's been raining for a week, so I'm not in the mood to play games!

So tell me already?

If this is about the refrigerator that got away I already heard about it! There will be hell to pay on that one.

Boss Bilkers get a phone call and leaves

Buddy

I hate that clown!

Jason

Try to forget it! You think I like these Jackasses? Where do they come from? Maybe Uranus!

He's a jackass, and the world is filled with them. We all know that. Look Buddy, if Bilkers didn't marry your sister Lucy she would still be in here busting bricks, Yea, but she is like a slave at home.

He saved her from a life of slavery! You have to give him that. He's your brother in law! You have to love him. He's putting food on your table, we all have people like that to deal with, and you know it. Taking his crap is part of the job here!

Buddy

The good Lord gave you a lot of sense. I wished I was

more like you sometimes.

Come on let's get the job done and get out of here.

Yeah!

~~~~~~~~~~~~~~~~~~~~

6

BAD NEWS TRAVELS FAST

After the workday as everyone is leaving work everyone is excited and talking about the lost refrigerator.

Just then out of the blue

Buddy

Boss Bilkers bought the farm! It happened this morning. He slipped on that gravel garden he has in front of his house and that's all she wrote! One less asshole to deal with!

A couple of people yelled back

No loss! The world is a better place for it.

Everyone is cheering and clapping even the security guards.

Before long everyone knew what happened. The gossip pipeline was going full tilt. Some people were even planning parties. He was one mean ass S.O.B. Most everyone hated his guts.

A detective is heard talking to a number of people.

Look it's no secret that he was rocking the cradle when he married Becky. She still looks good for her age. She was a Miss Ohio runner up!

What a looker!

Bilker stole her right from her Momma's arms. Anyway a lot of people see it that way!

The problem is that Boss had a million dollar life insurance policy and it was no secret that Becky was tired of him.

The kids are grown and maybe she wanted to start a new life in Bubba Heights or someplace like that. She told Boss she wanted a better life.

Problem was old Boss Bilkers was one of the cheapest sons of bitches ever to walk on this good earth, and most people knew it. Worked the hell out of people, then called them dumb asses while salting away serious money!

DETECTIVE HASSLEMAN

If it wasn't for the fact that I'm the only detective on the case right now, and I know all these people, I might just say the hell with it.

He got what he deserved! Most people will tell you

that!

Still and all it's my job to find out if he was knocked off or it was an accident. How many people do you know that water a rock garden early in the morning?

Well whatever. He had breakfast. The wife handed him his lunch and said, Boss Honey doesn't walk across my rock garden. He never listened to anybody, so walked across the garden where he slipped hit his head on one of those big rocks, and the rest is history.

Yet it is my job to investigate the whole thing, but right now it looks like an accident.

JAKE AND PINBALL BILL TALKING

Jake

Pinball did you hear that?

Pinball Bill

Yeah man. Looks like the old lady finally got the old bastard. I heard she tried before, but watering those stones in the morning with all that moss on them. Well sooner or later it was bound to happen.

Jake

Well Yeah!

Most of us know that cheap Jackass wouldn't even take her out to a movie or dinner. He worked the hell out of her as well at the factory. He had no sense of mercy or fair play.

Well she is free now! And still looks good. The guys are going to make a try for her now, especially how she will get bank rolled by that insurance policy.

SUSAN ROCKCREEK

When I drive by sometimes late at night I can see Becky ripping that double wide apart looking for the money that Boss Bilkers was thought to hide.

The way she is going I'll bet you'll see her driving a new car. That piece of crap she bought with her own money five years ago, well that will be gone the same way old man Bilkers went. Right to the scrap yard.

JAKE

I know! And good for her. If she wasn't such an old dog I'd make a play for her myself. Rumor is that she plans to move up to Bubba Heights when the money starts rolling in.

Well anyway that is where all the people want to live, and I can't blame them. If you have the money why not?

Look everyone knows it is one of the best places to hang your hat if you got the money for it. Looks like she does now!

^^^^^^^^^^^^

7

DOUG SLUGS MAKES THE MOVE

Well it finally happened!

Doug and Judy Slugs were able to get enough cash together to move out of the city. Their dream house was up on the hill in Bubba Heights.

Now they were going to be able to do what most everyone at the big factory wanted to do; move to Bubba Heights! That is the place where the junior Yuppies lived. Want to be movie star, and every fat cat jackass on planet earth wanted set up housekeeping with some fashion babe if they could nail one down.

A dream come true. The Slugs both work at the big plant. They saved their pennies for years, now it was their turn to live the high life up in the mountains. It was their turn to look down on the slave class and say; "We made it! Screw you little people! We hit one for the Gipper!"

Whenever anyone makes the move to Bubba Heights everyone else gets as jealous as hell and after that on Monday morning depression sets in for the new workweek.

After that life goes on.

Jake and some of the other guys have their eye on the girls with the best bank accounts. Jake is saving every nickel; he wants to get to Bubba Heights just like the rest of them. He knows the economy is taking a turn for the worse. He wonders if he will ever get up there one of these days?

He has dated Janet Buckman. Her old man is a war vet and mean as hell. He owns a landscaping business. Jake you often talk about tying the knot with Janet and hoping the old Man will spring for the down payment on one of those mountain houses in Bubba Heights.

Jake

Look guys I've been busting balls for years. I want to move up to Bubba Heights to. I don't care if they test those rocket engines up on the mountain!

They only test them once a month or so. It's a small price to pay for living up on the mountain. Everyone would be happier if they could finally get a home in Bubba Heights.

Pinball Bill

Jake we got to get back to work!

It's good to have dreams. They help us get through the day. By the way did anyone ever nail you guys for that appliance screw up? I heard several people were injured and it cost thousands of dollars!

Jake

No man we off on that one. Remember loose lips sink ships! We're laying low for a while.

By the way this weekend the Bigfoot expedition. Everyone is looking forward to it!

Pinball Bill

Yeah! Me to!

This is the largest group we ever put together. Think we'll see any UFOs out there. I heard Bigfoot sometimes has been seen getting off of them.

Jake

Look! Who the hell knows? Bring your cameras and stuff. Tell Bobbie to bring her binoculars. Tell everyone we will meet at John Crane's. That yuppie clown knows a lot about all of this. I'm beginning to like that nerd. People have a way of rubbing off on you. Try to keep things low key if you can.

Another thing; just because the Slugs moved up to Bubba Heights, it don't mean they won't go with us, so contact them!

STEVE MEETS SUSAN

I think it was around noon in Mary's coffee shop that Steve came in to buy something when he accidentally bumped into a gal coming out of the place.

Steve

Excuse me! I'm so sorry.

Susan

It's all right.

Steve

My name is Steve

Susan

I'm Susan

After the meeting they begin talking for a while. Then he tells her he is a cop from southern California; however, he was born and lived not far from here, and he is here on vacation visiting family.

Steve

Can I invite you to dinner sometime?

Susan

Okay.

Susan writes down her phone number and they go their separate ways.

~~~~~~~~~~~~~~~~~~~~~~~~

8

THE LOST STOVE

Rumors are still circulating about who lost that refrigerator up on the hill.

News just came in that the death of Boss Bilkers was accidental, and this opens the door for both Mrs. Bilkers and the live girlfriend Becky to move up in the world. Together they bought a beautiful place with a view and a swimming pool, and plan to pay cash for the house.

Looks like a lot of people are making the move out of the valley and finding a place to nest up in Bubba Heights. Jake and his buddies are waiting for their chance to get up in the world, but after that lost refrigerator. You know that big industrial unit that weighted as much as truck; they may be waiting a little longer.

JAKE

Hey guys the coast is clear. I have a friend that will pay us to move a stove up to Bubba Heights. We have to do it tonight after work! What do you say?

OWEN

Yeah we can do it no problem. How about right after dinner?

JAKE

Sounds like a plan!

Later that evening the guys get a hold of Sunny Brickman and Hoss Williams. They pick up and put in the truck. The guy hiring them starts telling stories and giving them beers. An hour goes by and then Jake says; "Let's move the damn thing I have to get home sometime.

Thank God I'm still single else there would be hell to pay.

They drove off heading for the mountain. Only one problem. They have a few beers and talked for a while, and they forgot to tie the stove down. Well there you have it.

What happened next was that when they rounded that last curve near the top the stove danced its way out of the truck and took on a life of its own.

It was just getting dark when the stove picked up speed on its way down the mountain. It knocked several cars off the road. Thank the good Lord nobody went over the side. After that it broke through a rusted out section of guardrail and took off in the air like a bird. You could see it up there for a few seconds then it just vanished.

The next day on the front page of the paper there was a picture of this stove sitting in this guy's bathroom right on the toilet. What a mess it was. There was a hole in the roof and the damages were in the thousands. When the guy was on TV he said, "I thought it came from outer space with all those flying saucers buzzing us and all!

They put out fliers and everything trying to find out who owned this stove, but nobody was talking. This was the second time, and everyone knew there would not be a third.

Well people felt sorry for him, but we knew we had to keep quiet, because loose lips sink ships!

Well after that day we all realized unless we were more serious about most everything we weren't going to get to Bubba Heights. And that meant so much to every one of us.

OWEN

Look guys if we are going to make some spare cash we have to be more careful before we hurt someone or get sued.

They all agree.

^^^^^^^^^^^^^^^^^^^^^^^

9

LIFE IN BUBBA HEIGHTS

I guess it was about a month after we lost that stove; early one morning we met a gal named Gina Coldpenny. Gina wanted to talk to us about buying a four-unit apartment building.

It was the one that had some minor damage from the last earthquake here. It nearly missed the last mudslide, and people say it had the luck of the Irish. You see a big house on one side slide down the hill and a store on the other side took a ride as well. This place seemed to have at least some bedrock under it.

Mrs. Coldpenny sells real estate, and had met Doug through the deal he made buying his place. Of course Doug told her about all of us. If we could pull this off, then we could realize our dream of moving to Bubba Heights.

Bubba Heights is a place where blue-collar workers can feel like that finally have made it in life. It's a mountain suburb about the valley, and it has its place in the big picture of life. When a factory worker is able to buy property up here and live that means something.

Some people are happy living down in the valley with all the buildings, noise, and pollution. Achieving the goal of making it to Bubba Heights is what it's all about in these parts. It's the American Dream. Two turkeys in the oven, three cars in the garage, and a house full of every kind of crap you can imagine. That's what people in these parts want.

She worked up a plan and the four of us used every penny we had to make it all happen. Two months later we were living in Bubba Heights. Our place didn't have the great view, but we made it. Then if we went up on our roof we could see the Pacific Ocean, so how cool is that?

From our roof we could see Becky's new place. Her and Old Boss Bilkers girl friend were living good. Both had new boyfriends; they waved back one evening. I guess a lot of people from the plant were living higher off the hog these days. If only that jackass Boss Bilkers could see how his old lady is spending his money these days, but I guess that will never happen.

Far in the distance you can see the Reagan Library on a clear day. A wonderful place to live. Well I bought in and so did Owen and TK Bird. The Bucket family bought the last unit. I worked with them for years and know them well.

We are all hoping life will be better for us all up here, and you know something; things are already getting better, so there you have it!

Actually once we settled in we realized life would be

different. We were somebody know. We would get some respect.

We started to spend evenings on the roof. We had a big Ghetto Blaster we would take up there, and we installed a makeshift shelter where we set up our outdoor cooking grill and picnic table.

Each night we sat after dinner study the other mountain for those fabled UFO's people see over there. We hoped to get a glimpse of Bigfoot as well. We spent hours up there studying everything.

We were making new friends and we stated holding our own UFO meeting in the basement. It was large and just had a few washers and dryers down there. We met every other Saturday and a lot of people came.

Sure some had real crazy stories, but we listened. We watched UFO movies and shared coffee and treats. It was a good time. Problem with life is if something is good it don't last long, and if it's boring it never seems to end. So like they say in Hollywood; "take your lumps and get on with it!"

Now that we are here we have to learn to adjust. Yesterday we read the flyer that that the company Rocket Flats was going to resume testing for the next six months. When we lived down in the valley you could hear the test, and when they performed night test you could see fire on the mountain, but now we were living closer to where that place was located.

Nobody can stop the test. They are mostly for the

space program. Then in six months it is said they are closing the place down for good.

The problem is we are facing six months of hell. Here's another thing we found out now that we have moved in. They use to test atomic rockets there back in the sixties. Some people will tell you; once in a blue moon you'll see a bat or a raccoon that glows in the dark. It has mostly been cleaned up, but it's like anything else in life. You can never get it all.

Now that we have moved up here making a dream of a lifetime come true the question is if paradise has so many problems why would you want to stay here?

I guess we will tough it out.

We can't afford to move again, so we decided to hang tough, because there are a lot of good things up here as well. After all we still have to work in the valley

Then it's like they say; "like goes on, and so will we!"

Just because you see a bat that glows in the dark every now and then doesn't mean you throw in the towel!

I guess like everyone else up here we will wait and see. For now life is better and I'll take that as a sign of better things to come.

^^^^^^^^^^^^^^^^^^^^^^

10

ROCKETS FLATS BEGINS TESTING

A place up in the mountains is known as Rocket Flats by the locals, and the testing of rocket engines up there is believed to cause several minor earthquakes. When you hear one of those things being tested it sounds like like thunder and echoes across these mountains. Although they don't test that much; they still run test now and then. The people around these parts hate it.

About two weeks ago they ran a short test. Every animal withing fifty miles was on the run included a large number of birds. Word is they will soon close down this facility, but it has not happened as yet.

Jerry Fields a family friend works up there, and usually gives us a heads up when a test is going to take place. He is an electrician and knows a lot, but is sworn to secrecy. Jerry understands that the Bigfoot that live in these mountains have thrown rocks at the place several times, but it is all keep on the quiet.

The state has a law if you harm a Bigfoot you could be fined and face prison time. Most people in these parts know that! Steve growing up near here knows that as well.

Rumors around here say that the Spanish have placed gold some place in this mountain range, but although many people have looked for it nobody has found anything.

Generally life goes on here pretty much normal. The fishermen go out on their boats, farmers farm, and the factories are cranking up production every day. Of course timber is being taken by the logging companies. Life in general seldom sees anything strange, but if you go deep in those mountains you see and hear a lot of strange stories.

I have heard my share and I know Steve's folks. He has heard his share of the stuff that goes on around here. One story that floats around is that somebody in these parts has a map and knows where that gold is hidden, but nobody has been able to find out anything, and a lot of people have tried.

Early one Saturday morning the test begins. Right after eight A.M. a huge roar is heard on the mountain. It's like an earthquake. Things are falling off their shelves and everyone is running for their lives.

The good news if you can call it that is the test only last between ten and thirty seconds! After that they blow a loud horn and sound the all clear. Once the smoke clears things pretty much get back to normal. Well mostly dogs can be heard barking and moaning for another fifteen minutes or so.

I guess it's just the price you have to pay for living here in paradise. Sometimes I think; who the hell needs it anyway?"

Maybe I was better off living with the muskrats down in the valley?

Who knows what will happen next' but things always seem to go in three's. I hope I'm wrong and yet I have this strange feeling about these mountains. Always did, but lately I've been getting that sick feeling.

I guess we will all have to wait and see?

∧∧∧∧∧∧∧∧∧∧

11

THINGS THAT GO BUMP

That night after the rocket tests it was pretty quiet. You could hear crickets in the hills and the moon was out. At our UFO meeting in the basement we had a speaker from NASA. He told us how we planned to go back to the moon and see if anyone was home in 2025.

The problem was most of the club, and for that matter maybe half the population of the world already knew advanced alien spacecraft were already here!

Hello!

It was fun anyway, and you always learn something new. Roger decided to attend our meetings one a month. We liked that. After the meeting while sitting up on the roof looking for UFO's and watching the hills for a possible glimpse the big forest people, we decided to go on a big adventure up on that forbidden mountain.

We don't go over to that mountain near the presidential Library anymore. When you go over there on one of those trails you reach the summit with the big cross and you can see out over the Pacific Ocean.

Boy what a view that is!

Well one day I was taking my early morning hike with several friends like we usually do a few times a week. When we reached a place about to thirds of the way up suddenly several governmental agents wearing black jumped out in front of us.

First Agent

Stop right there! Where in the hell do you think you are going?

Owen

Hey! What in the hell is going on! We always come up on a hike to see the ocean!

Second Agent

Well not today! You see all the ex-presidents are meeting at the library today, so you'll have to head back down. Sorry you know how it is!

Pinball Bill

Yeah well you guys ain't doing your job! You're not guarding the other path that comes up here!

First Agent

What are you talking about?

Pinball   Bill

Look dude, just around that bend is another way up here. Here people could sneak right past you, and then you'd be in a world of crap. Better get some people over there!

Second Agent

He gets on the radio

Then yells get going! By the ways thanks!

After that they walked back down.

∧∧∧ ∧∧∧ ∧∧∧

You have all kinds of things out here. There in Box Canyon they have those old western towns where all the old movie stars filmed westerns. President Reagan made movies down there. The place is famous.

Once Rocket Flats folds up shop and moves on, then life will be better up here. Well anyway we hope it goes that way. I guess like all things time will tell.

Buddy

Yeah that was something! On Bigfoot Mountain we should have a clear trail right to the summit. Few people go up there anymore.

Owen

I know! People have vanished up there never to be seen again!

Jake

We're not going to let that stop us are we?

I mean we'll take some firepower and maybe a little firewater with us. We have a couple of big lights and we'll take all the cameras. Maybe we'll get lucky and see something. Just think of the pictures and video we could get. Man we'd be famous!

Owen
Yeah! Get on TV becomes famous Bigfoot and UFO hunters. Get on one of those shows.

Jake

Well yeah! Let's do it!

The group plans to go and spend the weekend on Bigfoot Mountain and see what they can come away with from the trip. They start planing everything that night.

They go to church the next morning and after dinner plan the whole thing out. They invite Judy the factory secretary who has an uncanny interest in Bigfoot, and Susan a gal that Jake has been dating when he can find the time. She has little interest in UFOs or Bigfoot, but likes Jake so she agrees to go along

The following Saturday morning they pack up and head up the mountain.

Nine people in all headed up the mountain path. A lot of people told them not to go, but they have been in a few tough spots, so they figured they could pull it off.

It's like Owen said, "better to do something even if it's wrong rather than sitting around waiting for a forest fire to get your ass a moving."

I guess he had a point there!

Well what happened next is that we left early. We drove over and parked at the base of the mountain. As we started up the trail we had a strange feeling. All of us seem to feel it, and we talked about it a while. You know one of those weird feelings you just can't seem to shake off.

Still and all we pressed on up the trail. As we moved up the mountain that morning we could still hear traffic on the roads in the area. That was weird in itself.

A few hours later we were deep in the forest. We could hear these strange whistling sounds. Some people say that it's the sounds of Bigfoot communicating with each other. Then we saw several deer running just ahead. There was a lot of wildlife up there, and you could sense it.

We were surprised to find this huge clearing about two thirds of the way up. Owen says he saw something big jump behind a tree. That spooked me.

Owen

Hey guys; there's something over there take a look! It just jumped behind that tree!

Both Judy see the same thing.

JUDY

I saw it! Big with kind of red-brown hair!

JAKE

Well let's check it out! We're not going to find anything if we don't do something!

OWEN

You got a point! Let's do it!

As they got near the place they heard something big moving through the trees. They didn't go any further.

Then Jake yelled!

JAKE

Look at that!

As they walked on a while they came upon a camp. It

had the look of being abandoned. It appeared to be a place where drugs were being processed. There were a couple of piles of what looked like drugs. Some were cut in squares, and there were several different kinds.

OWEN

Dude something bad happened here! Look blood on that tree, and on some of those packages. I don't think this happened to long ago either!

JAKE

Buddy grab someone and haul ass down this mountain and bring Detective Hassleman up here. Tell him to come alone if he can. I want him to see this for himself. He'd never believe us after we clowned around so much during the investigation.

We'll be right here.

BUDDY

On my way! I'll take Hoss!

JAKE

Well make sure it's all right with Betty!

BUDDY

I'll take her too!

While they sat there thinking about the whole thing Jake decided to walk out to the other side of the plain. It looked like it was a long way, but he decided it would be hours before they got back.

He takes Owens and tells the rest of the party to stay put till someone shows up. One guy turns on a radio. The rest are eating snacks and drinking water.

JAKE

Let's go Owen. Let's try to figure out what the hell is going on here!

OWEN

Yeah. Should I load the gun now?

JAKE

I don't see why not?

Don't shoot yourself in the foot, and whatever you do please don't get stuck on stupid! We have enough trouble here as it is!

They move on across the field where a few rolling hills

are. After a while they climb this small hill and from there they can see the Pacific Ocean.

OWEN

Man Jake this place is God's country!

JAKE

That it is Owen. I'll tell you something else we are not alone up here. We're being watched right now.

OWEN

Well who do you think is watching us?

JAKE

Well it's not those drug dealers. They would have already been on us. Whoever is watching us must have killed those people back at the camp. I think those big forest men must have their home up here some place, and they took out that drug operation.

It's just a feeling. You know a guess.

Must of come in at night or during the morning when it was just getting light. They wouldn't have expected it then. They removed everything. They didn't leave much for the cops I can tell you that!

OWEN

Since you put it that way it seems to make some sense! We should get the hell out of here and head back!

JAKE

Maybe you're right. You've been right once or twice before as I recall!

They look around and start heading back. Both of them hear whistling sounds in the trees and see branches shaking every now and then. They make their way back just in time to see a Helicopter land in the clearing where Detective Hassleman and two other cops get off. Jake and Owen watch as the chopper leaves the mountain.

Walking over they shake hands with the detectives.

JAKE

Look detective we came up here looking to find evidence of the Bigfoot, and at night we were hoping to see UFOs. I know that sounds a little crazy to you, but then we are serious UFO hunters. We have meetings and everything!

DETECTIVE HASSLEMAN

Well not as strange as you might think. I've seen my share of crap too. Not only on the job, but in these mountains. Maybe someday I'll talk to you about it, but this ain't that day!

What have we got here?

Jake

Well Detective best I can tell looks like a drug bust or drug exchange gone bad. Hard to know. We came upon this place and took a look. After that I sent two guys down when I couldn't get you on the phone. Do ever answer it?

12

THE SECOND DETECTIVE

Look kid I can't even get a hold of him half the time and I'm his partner. He hates phones!

Detective Hassleman sealed the area and told them to move on or get off the mountain. Their choice. Well since they were staying the night they decided to move deeper in the mountains near the coast. They figured from up there at night they just might get some UFO video, so that's what they did!

I guess it was about four in the morning when it happened. A large ship came down and landed not far from where we were. It was too incredible to consider but there she was sitting in the field giving off a brilliant display of colors to our amazement.

It was one of those things that you don't see every day!

The most amazing part was that a large door open on the side of the ship and after some kind of vapors streaming off a group of Bigfoot creatures came walking out and looking around.

That put the fear of God in us I can tell you that!

Well we all stayed hunkered down not moving a muscle. The a group of the Big forest creatures walked up and walked into the ship. Moments later the big saucer made a whining sound and shoot straight up in the air and headed out over the ocean. It was out of sight in mere seconds.

What do you make of that?

Hey we got some pictures, and after showing them at the club they somehow vanished along with our CD's. Who could have done that? Maybe we had a debunker in our club, but we may never know who it was.

We are more careful these days.

After that we got strange phone calls, and strange people came around a lot! What do you make of it all? One thing is for sure we don't intend to go back up there anytime soon.

Another thing that campsite where the drugs were; well the detective told us it never happened. UFO nuts tend to get carried away, so it was all swept under the tug. Hell who knows why?

I told to Hazzleman several times. This is what he told me; "you boys have enough problems. How would you like us to open up that closed case on your Boss? How do we know that after all you had something to do with his death? We don't do we! Have you boys ever heard of the expression; "let sleeping dogs alone."

Well there is a lot of truth in that. Go fly your UFOs, and hunt for Bigfoot, but as far as anything else goes you don't know nothing! Clear enough! I got to go!

∧∧

13

ROSS WINDFIELD PRIVATE EYE

A private eye shows up in the city asking all kinds of questions. Some people think that he was sent by the big insurance company. Yet nobody knows for sure who he is working for.

He met with some federal agents in town and has been to the police station several times. All anybody knows is that he has serious law enforcement connections.

Ross meets Pinball Bill crossing the street by the main traffic light in town.

ROSS

Sir may I ask you a few questions. It seems a lot of strange things are going on around here, and my job is to investigate.

Ross introduces himself and so does Pinball. Then Ross ask Pinball a few questions after inviting him for lunch.

Ross

Tell me about the area and what you think is going on here?

Pinball talks to him for about twenty minutes and then;

Alright I'm getting the picture. What do you know about this guy Steve?

Pinball Bill

Well I know his whole family. My older brother graduated from high school with him. He grew up her. He was in the military and after that he became a cop in southern California. Right know he is up here on a vacation for a while. What is the problem? Is he guilty of something?

Ross

No not at all! My job is to find out what I can about the people around here. You see I've been hired to investigate a possible crime in the area. The more I know about the people here the easier my job will be.

Pinball Bill

Oh I see! Well I hope that helps you, and look me up if you need anything else.

Each go their separate ways.

The detective leaves to check on other people that might know something.

~~~~~~~~~~~~~~~~~~

14

PARADISE COMES WITH PROBLEMS

Finding paradise on earth isn't always what you think it is, because paradise like everything else comes with its own share of problems. It's just you seldom know that up front. You find out about the problems later. After you move there, or sign the papers.

Sure a lot of people think that paradise is a true paradise. Most things look good at a distance. The problems come in after you have been there a while. It may still be a paradise, and yet most of the time a paradise that is here on the earth may not be all that you thought that it was.

Well shortly after coming down off Bigfoot Mountain the ground started to shake. Turns out we were having another earthquake! I began thinking about our some apartment complex. I was at work when it happened. It lasted nearly a minute. The factory suffered some damage.

I punched out got in my car and headed up the mountain. I could see Owen in my rear view mirror I waved and headed home. I began wondering what kind of a paradise we were living in. They were still fighting that forest fire down in the valley.

What else could happen?

I should have kept my mouth shut that day because the sky clouded up and we had one of the worst thunderstorms in memory. About the time I got home it was pouring buckets off the side of the house.

Then it happened!

The power went out!

We were in the dark. I never bought a flashlight or candles, but you can bet I will after this. It rained and it rained. After it got dark it rained some more.

We awake late in the night to this rumbling sound. Then we realized something bad was happening, but didn't know what!

Suddenly we heard screams and heard a whooshing sound followed by a crash.

PINBALL

Hey guys somebody's house just slide off the mountain. How safe is this place?

JAKE

Calm down! Everyone it will be all right! They had special anchors put in this building.

OWEN

I'm wondering why the hell we moved up here now! I mean this is real scary! Where is your girlfriend hiding I haven't seen here.

SUSAN

I'm fine guys. I'm hiding behind the couch with the dog!

Well in the morning they went out and noticed two houses were missing from the street. The sun had come out, and everyone was going about their business.

Nobody was seriously injured that night

The next day we found out we lost several of our neighbors. We came out of reasonably well, but when you live in paradise you expect a little more!

The following work week a lot of people told us that we would have been better off to have stayed in the valley. After all sucking in a little pollution and getting hassled in traffic was better than riding in your house down a mountain mud slide.

Maybe that had a point, but we were already up there now, so we had to make the best of it. Week after week a siren would sound up in the mountains and you would hear the sound of those rocket engines being tested.

Every time they ignited for a test every house in Bubba Heights would get some kind of a shaking. One house nearly collapsed on a Saturday afternoon. It sat there at a funny angle. The people had to leave.

Most of us knew they were closing the planet and they were trying to get in as many test as possible. I even went up to the front gate with a large group of people in protest, but it didn't do much good. Nobody even came out to talk to us, so there you have it!

Another things every now and then you could feel a slight tremor in the ground. When you pay good money to live in paradise you expect it to be a paradise!

We were getting up in the world, but sometimes I wonder if it was doing any of any good. My old boss was died slipping and falling on the slippery stones would laugh if he see what happened to us. The Boss's poor widow and his girlfriend lost their garage and one car in the mudslide. I talked to them about it and they are real upset. Well who wouldn't be?

I guess paradise is a lot like everything else no matter where you live it has its ups and its downs, and in more ways than one! You just have to learn to live with it taking the good with the bad, and having enough common sense to know the difference.

What shakes me up the most is simply knowing that what goes up must come down. I hope we don't have to move back down in the valley. I heard that a big lay off is coming down the pike.

15

WHAT GOES UP

When the economy gets a black eye the people usually get kicked on their ass! It's just the way it works! When the house of cards comes down people get hurt in every imaginable way.

I guess it was about a week after the mudslide and all that other crap that both my friends and myself got our lay off slips. We knew would could hold on for a short while, but the handwriting was on the wall.

We had to bail out and move back down in the valley. We talked it all over and soon knew we couldn't keep paying the high cost of these rental apartments. Then we weren't alone in this either. A lot of them would have to take a fall.

What would we do now!

Hell would could anybody do?

One thing was for sure we had to do something! We tried selling a book and a home movie on UFOs and our encounter with the Bigfoot creatures, but in this economy nobody was buying. We couldn't even give them away.

We understood that America was at a point in its history where it was maxed out on stuff. Everybody in the country already has enough stuff to depress them for the next decade!

I think we are entering a time where people are not going to buy anything more than what they have to have. It will hurt all of us, because we are all use to having a ton of crap in our house and garage. Not to mention having a storage bin loaded to the garage door!

Where do we go from here? What do you do when you can't pay for anything, but you have everything? You can't give it away. Good Will been known to turn stuff down!

The handwriting was on the wall. It was downhill from here. And it looks like a lot of us are going the way of the mudslide. Who knows what will happen when we hit bottom?

Bum City and a welfare dime might be just ahead for a lot of us? Americans are a resilient lot. Maybe we will pull out, but at what cost and how long? Looks like a lot of people will be filing for chapter seven, or chapter eleven in bankruptcy court.

Good times and bad times, and all the in between times makes life what it is. Maybe I heard it in a song some years ago, but whatever it's the way real life seems to works. We all get our share of mudslides along the way.

^^^^^^^^^^^^^^^^^^^^^^^^^^

16

THE SATURDAY NIGHT ROCKET TEST

Most everyone knew that a big rocket engine was going to take place soon, but this Saturday is when it will happen. That is tomorrow night. The spokesman for the rocket testing lab has issued a warning that it will happen as scheduled at ten on the next Saturday evening.

Most everyone has their own views about it, and there has been a number of rumors that the place is going to close down soon. This will put a lot of local people out of work. People hate the place, but a lot of them have good jobs there.

On Friday night most people were out doing things. Susan was asked to dinner by Steve, and they were at the local drive in when the scheduled test time arrived. While in the car a siren sounded loudly. Steve told Susan he had forgotten about that rocket test. Then the roar started and echoed across the mountains. It was so loud they couldn't hear the movie at all. It lasted for about a minute, and then there was a loud explosion.

Everyone wondered what happened!

Steve yelled out; "They blew the damn thing up the jackasses!" He started the car and they drove off.

Steve

Let's go over to my place it is quiet and we can watch a movie in TV.

Susan

Sounds good. Boy was that loud! I guess it will be in the paper tomorrow?
Can we stop at that all night store and pick up a few things?

Steve

No problem! Let's not get too excited by it all. They probably got it shut down. They s[pend a quiet night together.

The following morning word about it is everywhere. Fire trucks were there all night. Half of the pant burned down. People are saying the plant is closed permanently.

17

PING PONG TEMPORARY SERVICE

For a while we had some fun, but later that summer we got our eviction notice. A lawyer I know told me he lives with shut off and eviction notices. He pays everything at the last possible minute.

You see; it's all about deny and bottleneck tactics. The overall strategy being you live you way you have always lived and enjoy what you have, because you still have it!

Look let's say someone is going to promise you the moon through some economic program or something like that. The problem comes in when you try to negotiate the bottleneck set up by the system that only allow a certain amount of people to get what was promised.

Most people are caught up in the bottleneck, and therefore either get tired of waiting and give up, or they find something else to do. That way everything comes out looking great, and a few people are helped.

Few that they may be, but in the big picture it looks like a great program that worked. Because the wax dummies that follow the plan can always parade a few lottery winners and then get on with the next thing.

Well that's what the lawyer told me. I could go on, but I think that you get the picture1

Sure he is a friend, but he needs cover too. He still has a nest of birds to feed, and when the chow hounds scream out, then you have to have some food. God forbid you become their next meal and that has happened too.

What more can you say?

Well what happened next I got together with my friends and we went out looking for work shortly before our benefits ran out. We had to find something we got our three day notice from the Sheriff's office. We were fast running out of delays and creating reverse bottlenecks to stop the system from beating us on the head.

What we did next was to get a few temporary gigs from Ping-Pong Temporary Service. That's a large temporary service that will put you to work and steal your rights. If you don't full fill the day's assignment they will bust you down to minimum wage. If you mouth off to any employee you can be terminated in a New York minute. Well you get the picture.

Our group found a second story rental. Not a lot of room, but with five people and four rooms it was not our idea of a good time. Maybe you can see where I'm going with this?

After that we bounced around a lot from one temp job

to another job. When you work for a temp service to take your lumps and bounces as well!

Life is like war!

If you never learned that, then you are in a world of hurt!

Money is like war!

If you have never learned that, then you are in a bigger world of hurt!

People get hurt and they take tough losses all the time.

Sure, you have to take your losses along with your assets, but after you weigh both in the balances what is the outcome?

I guess it is different for everyone.

Even Doug Slugs and his old lady lost their ass in this economic down turn. He meets with the guys after coming to the UFO meeting for the first time.

∧∧∧∧∧∧∧∧∧∧∧

DOUG

Guys I'm sorry I waited so long to join. I promised you all so many times. It's just that I had my head in the clouds under the economy kicked me in the ass! Then I woke up. I was on a yuppie get rich quick trip. Now it seems to be all over. Please don't hold it against me!

OWEN

I hear you dude!

JAKE

Look! Times they are a changing, and faster than any of us can keep up with. We all have to start thinking of living and working together, because none of us can make it on his or her own anymore.

Oh sure Boss Bilker's harem can make it. Because they were lucky enough to get a bundle after he took that fall on those wet stones! You will always have your lottery winners in this world few though that they be!

For most of us it's a battle everyday trying to stay alive. Life is mean as hell, but that don't mean you throw in the towel. People are as evil as the day is long filled with con and selfish motives, but that doesn't mean you hate people and ignore them.

We are all in this together.

Look life is a lot like chapters in a book! Each one is a puzzle until you have read it. Then you get some idea of how to move on in your book from there.

Well I think you see what I'm saying guys!

18

LOOK MOMMA NO BRAKES

A few days later when the guys got together.

OWEN

Look I have been waiting to tell you all something!

I got the truck repaired and I have an order to take an industrial refrigerator down to the valley. A restaurant near Box Canyon. I need two of you to help. We can make a good buck on this and it won" take all day!

Don't volunteer all at once!

JAKE

You know I'm in. T need the money badly!

HOSS

Are you sure the truck is working good?

Will you double-check the ropes? If you will I'm in.

PINBALL

Yeah! I'll give it a shot!

I hope this goes better than the last time. I'm nearly shell shocked from the last run.

OWEN

Cool your heels dudes. Everything is fine. A piece of cake and we'll each get a nice piece of change out of it. I figure less than half of the day and that's it.

They all head for home. Tomorrow is Saturday and the guys got up early to get this job over with. After coffee and donuts they load the unit on the truck. Then doubled tied it down. It wasn't going anywhere period.

They went in for another coffee. Jake looked out the window and notice the wind came up hard blowing crap everywhere. The lady behind the corner said, "here we go again another San Anna wind storm. And this one looks pretty darn bad."

After coffee they all got in the truck and headed down the mountain. The wind was mean as hell blowing vehicles all over the road that morning.

JAKE

This is one rough ass ride I can hardly hold her!

Hang on boys the fun is just starting!

Wow, wow! The brakes are gone!

Hang on for dear life I can't hold her!

PINBALL

Grab the emergency!

JAKE

It's broke old buddy! We are screwed!

^^^^^^^

They all hung on for dear life as the truck picked up a decent speed. They were flying low! Several cars went out of control and they ran a pickup truck with two out timers off the mountain.

They were all plenty scared as the truck failed to make the next turn and skidded sideways busting through the guardrail. They were going downhill now dodging big pine trees. Suddenly they high this flat spot and went flying through the air.

They were all hanging on for dear life and screaming as

the truck hit the river in a huge belly slam! Now they were going down stream and wind seemed to pick up speed.

Then the truck got stuck on a low place in the river. They all climbed out and got on the hood and roof. They were hanging on for dear life when the first rescue fire truck arrived.

After almost an hour all of them thanks to the rescue people were on dry land. The truck began to slide and went down stream toward the Pacific Ocean neither it nor the refrigerator were ever seen again.

They barely escaped with their lives.

OWEN

Boys I'm getting out of the hauling business! That was the last straw. I mean I can't go through anymore of this.

JAKE

I'm going to have to second that!

19

A FRESH START

There are times in life when everything you have or everything you know just seems to slide down hill, and you are left with nothing.

You find yourself spinning your wheels and going in circles never able to get off the wheel. A bad economy and a lot of problems. You feel like dog crap and depression comes along and kicks you in the ass.

Where do you go from here?

Some people say that living life to the fullest is the experience of a lifetime. I'd like to believe that. Maybe it's true?

Some people call us hero's because we have had so many adventures, and other people call us complete horse's ass's. Maybe we are some place in between, but what do I know?

I'm lucky to be alive at all!

Sure we been through some crap. I can't deny that. Still and all life goes on! Maybe it is time for a fresh start. A change of direction. Re-inventing who and what we are?

You know what I mean!

Maybe if we stop trying to find the good life it will come
Along and find us. Maybe our approach was wrong! We have to try something new and different. You know like going in business and selling used cars. That's a good racket.

OWEN

Guys I came up with a plan!

JAKE

All right Owen what! This better be good!

And no more hauling crap!

OWEN

Used cars we are going to open a car lot and sell cars! The insurance money and what I have saved we can get a license and open a small lot. If it does well, then we are back in business!

Who knows in a few years we'll be back up on the mountain? The rocket testing facility will be history; I think in a couple of years things will be better. Maybe the recession will be over as well!

Why not?

What have we got to lose anyway?

JAKE

Sounds like a plan! Let's do it!

We can hire Susan, and since you have been dating that gal from the factory maybe we can have a double wedding, but first we have to put them to work. You know break them into the business. Well Susan is already broke in.

Let's not get ahead of ourselves though. The best part of life is letting it happen!

You know what I think?

We have done some things that most people will never get to do. The problem is no matter how good it is you can't stay there forever. Life for all of us is really about moving on. I guess it's like taking a ride down a river and fighting the current and the rapids. The rocks and the weather.

You just have to know when to get back in the boat, because there is always along section of river to run. It's just the way it is. You have taken the journey, because there is no other way to go.

20

LIFE GOES ON

OWEN

There is something you need to know!

Our friend Pinball is moving back to Cleveland. He said he had enough. His uncle in Parma has a job for him pulling muck out of Lake Erie or something like that!

His friend Parky Cleveland called him a few days ago. Well Parky is called Parky because no matter how he tried to get out of Cleveland; he always found himself parking his ass back in the city for one reason or another.

JAKE

We are going to miss him!

Things won't be the same anymore. Life has a way of changing so fast! All the fun and things we did; well I guess it's over.

You know when they called us back to the factory to work a week here and a week there I thought we would have that job for life. Now it looks like the factory is going to close its doors.

You know you're probably the best friend I have in this world. If you leave what will happen to me. Sure I'm getting married and I'll have children, but it's these times I'll always remember most.

It's all kind of sad when you think about it!

OWEN

Then don't think about it!

I'm not going anywhere. We are friends for life. You're like a brother to me. I never had any brothers. You know my five sisters. I love them all, but our friendship is special.

Let's keep it that way.

JAKE

Let's get started in the morning we got a lot of work to do. My uncle was a car salesman for thirty years. He said he would teach me every trick in the game. Including throwing quarters around the lot in the early morning.

JAKE

You know people will come and people will go, but if we can stay together as friends and business partners, well besides family it'll be all I'll need in this life!

OWEN

Don't forget we still have the UFO club and what have you! New people will come and life will go on, and I guess we will as well.

JAKE

See you in the morning!

21

FINDING THE MAP

The last Friday of every month the city hold a street wide flea market. Lucy and Judy have a large area out in front of their store. Lucy and Judy are two older divorcees who have owned the Frontier Antique shop for over fifteen years. They spend a better part of a year buying up stuff for the sale for places all around.

These gals will but up anything that they think will see. People come from as far away as a hundred miles for the big week end sale. This year they expect a large crown, and everyone has high hopes of making a few bucks.

This year here in the summer they are holding an all week end sale. The place is expected to be packed. Steve is planning to pick up some items to take back to L.A. He promised his four children and the wife that he would bring them back something from the big sale.

Today is the day of the big sale. Both homes and businesses are ready for the crowd. Everybody is hoping for a record sales year. Early in the morning you find Lucy and Judy out on the main street as well as many other people hoping for early sales.

People are now coming into the city from everywhere. Steve is out there shopping with the big crowd. When he gets to Lucy's place he sees a beautiful blue vase he thinks his wife will love, so he buys it and begins looking for a few other treasures for his kids.

While shopping he meets a gal named Jena Rockcreek. Her family owns a big ranch about twenty miles from here. She is a fine looking filly whose family owns a big horse farm.

Steve ask the lady if she would allow him to accompany her during the sale. He says he will buy her dinner after-wards, and she agrees. They spend the next few hours shopping and looking around. Then they go for dinner at a local dinner.

Just after dinner and some general conversation she notices some cloth in the vase that Steve had purchased; and says, "Steve you have something in that vase you bought. Steve looks in and pulls out a cloth folded up. He open it and to his surprise it looks like a treasure map. He quickly folds it back up.

Jena; you won't believe what this is! It's the lost treasure map of the hidden Indian cave that everyone has been looking for for years. When I was a kid people were talking about this map and looking for it, but nobody ever found it. People knew it exited because an old prospector had it and was showing it around back in the 1930'. Well that is the way I heard it.

Come on with me to my dad's house and we will see what he has to say about it. She agrees and they go in her car out to the family farm. Getting there he sees his day doing a few chores. I guess day didn't go again to the street fair. He seldom goes. My mom goes every year come rain or shine.

They greet a few people and go inside. A few minutes later Steve's dad comes in. Steve opens the map over coffee, and his dad studies it and say; son this is the real McCoy! And if this map is right the cave entrance is not far from the highway on the coast!

What should we do asks Steve? Well son a lot of people would kill to get this thing, so we have to be very careful. You know where that yuppie motorcycle gang got stoned by Bigfoot? Steve answers, "yeah, so what?" Then his dad says; "they were about a mile from this cave entrance according to the way I make this all out."

Steve yells out, "then let's go there!" "Not so fast son. First we have to be very careful and get a few people that we can really trust to go along. It all has to be done very carefully."

After reaching an agreement they all go their separate ways until Steve's dad decides on a time for a meet. Steve began to wonder who would be going along on this trip. I started to wonder about those big fellas up on the mountain. Then it came to me that they might have something to do with that the stoning of that motorcycle gang. Possibly they were just too close to the cave?

By the way my name is Jake Handley, and I was there.

I know the whole story, and I'm telling it to you. And for a number of good reasons.

~~~~~~~~~~~~~~~~~~

22

FINDING THE TREASURE CAVE

Now that Steve has found the map he talks it over with a few friends and decides on a plan to go there. The interesting thing is that the cave is shown to be about a mile or so from where the Bigfoot creatures threw stones at the motorcycle gang.

Steve has everyone meet him at a park not far from the place where the map says the cave is located.

STEVE

Good morning everyone!

We are about to find the hidden treasure cave. I have asked each of you to go with me because I know all of you and I trust you. Now when I call your name Jake with tell you more, and once we get the plan straight we will go there. I think it t will take just a couple of hours, so is everyone ready for the journey?

All reply, "yes let's go!

The group consist of;

Steve Eagleson
Jake Handley
Jerry Fields
Otis Crabtree
Susan Rockcreek
Becky Thornapple

About 10 in the morning they start walking toward the cave.

About two hours later they approach the place where the map says the cave is located.

At first they don't see any sign of it; however; after a search Becky find an opening to the big cave.

The group gathers and slowly enter the cave which turns out to be a large cavern once they walk inside of it.

After walking further in the group spots a small group of gold bars and some jewels laying around.

Everyone is gathering what they can carry, and then Steve tells them we shall go and come back another day.

Just as they are leaving shots ring out and a few hit near where they are standing. Then a voice yells at them, "come out in a single file and out what you have in a small pile in front of the cave."

The group is unarmed and has no choice but to comply. They walk out and put most everything down.

A VOICE YELLS OUT

You people leave here now and don't ever come back!

The group slowly leaves the area.

JUST THEN

The group sees large rocks being thrown at the men as they were trying to carry off the gold and jewelry. Several were killed immediately. The rest thrown down some of the stuff and tried to make a hasty exit from the place.

Some of the big creatures were hit, but they managed to kill or severely wound the group of men.

After that Steve and the others left the area knowing they were lucky to get out with their lives. They headed back to the meeting place.

STEVE

I don't know who those people are, but they won't be back. And we will never go back I'm sure. It appears that place is guarded by the Bigfoot. Who knows why?

Becky and Susan managed to keep several pieces of jewelry and Steve had held on to a small gold bar, so they came out of it all right. Nobody was hurt and they got a few things; however, it is doubtful that any of them will go there again.

23

MEETING CHIEF FLYING OWL

After everyone cooled down and they all got back to the city Steve decided he had enough of gold mining. Anyway he came out of there with one gold brick, and you know that had to be worth something.

STEVE

Look guys we at least found it and did our best. None of us got hurt. Sure I told hit in the shoulder; however, it is not serious, and the doc told me just take it easy for a while. The bullet went clean through, and he said it was just a flesh wound that would heal up quickly.

I guess all I can say is we solved a puzzle, and we know that cavern is large. Just maybe those Bigfoot creatures live in there. Whatever... life goes on.

Before they all leave Steve ask Susan for dinner. She accepts.

At the evening dinner a tall Indian walks over and ask if he can join them.

STEVE

Sure have seat!

The chief places an order and then begins talking to them.

CHIEF FLYING OWL

You know yo have uncovered a great mystery in these parts. Now a lot of people will try to get up there. The problem is that those big creatures will stop them. There may rooms of gold up there for all anyone knows.

STEVE

Well chief I'm not going up there anymore.

The chief smiles and says; that's good.

The chief winks at Steve perhaps he knows he got one gold bar, but he keeps quiet, and soon says good bye.

After dinner the couple leave and Steve walks her home.

24

STEVE GETS MARRIED

After going through all the excitement here in the city not far from the place known as Bubba Heights Steve ask Susan out for summer. Susan came here from Ohio. She was a runner up in the Miss Ohio contest couple of years ago. She came out here with her uncle and aunt who bought land not far from Bubba Heights.

Hoss and Betty Williams always wanted to move to northern California, and after a number of years were able to purchase five acres and a small farm house.

Susan's family lives back in the Cleveland area. Susan got her college degree from the Internet, and spends a lot of time on the net. She has a job with a Real Estate firm in the city.

Susan has dated a lot but has never married, She attends church and likes Steve. Now after all the things that have happened around here she thinks Steve is the man for her.

One beautiful morning Steve ask Susan out for breakfast. After they eat:

STEVE

Susan I have been wanting to talk to you. What I'm saying is would you marry me?

Susan

I accept !

They tell everyone and the married is scheduled for the following Fall.

Steve still has a brick of gold, and he has a real job. They talk everything over and decide to move up to Bubba Heights after the marriage.

25

POSTSCRIPT

Jake and his friend Owen went on to open a used car dealership and today they are doing well. Both are married and have teenage children. They both attend an Assembly of God church right there in the Semi Valley.

Boss Bilkers old lady re-married a Hollywood director and moved out of Bubba Heights. She never came back as far as anyone knows.

Becky repaired the garage and still lives up in Bubba Heights. She never married. She is doing well and goes out on fishing trips with a group see met on the Marina.

Doug Slugs and his wife have a big family and are doing well. They still live in Bubba Heights. They are good friends of a lot of the people we all knew that lost their jobs in the recession. Some call it a modified depression.

The Millkweeds and Bobbie Bilkers started a business together selling stuff made in China. They call it the Far East Outlet. We see them now and then. They buy cars from us when they need them.

Boss Darkcon and his wife still living in Bubba Heights. He's a travelling salesman these days. His wife owns a small store at the Mall.

Hoss and Betty Williams own and run a restaurant up in Bubba Heights called the Earthquake Dinner.

Finally Detective Benny Hassleman became the police Chief down the valley. His wife works at the Reagan library.

The rocket flats company closed its doors and left for Utah. The guys knew some of them. Nice people, but those rocket test were terrible. Ping-Pong Job Service closed its doors and left like a lot of other companies.

In time everything has a way of changing, maybe it was meant to be that way.

The End

BUBBA HEIGHTS

ALBERT JOHN PEEBLES

BUBBA HEIGHTS